THIRD
HAND
BOOKS

WALDEN POND

Patty Nash

Thirdhand Books
Columbia, Missouri
3rdhandbooks.com

Thirdhand Books LLC, Columbia, Missouri, 65201
www.3rdhandbooks.com
© 2024 by Thirdhand Books
Printed in the United States of America

Library of Congress Cataloging-in-Publication Data on File

ISBN (paperback): 978-1-949344-53-0
ISBN (ePub): 978-1-949344-54-7
1 2 3 4 5

Front cover image: :"Container ships President Truman (IMO 8616283) and President Kennedy (IMO 8616295) at San Francisco." California Publication of the National Oceanic & Atmospheric Administration (NOAA), USA. Public domain.

Cover design by Lindsey Webb.

Contents

Lübeck

Lübeck

The wheel of history is being turned

Terns skim the wetlands which are evaded by the tiller

The tiller is the lever which turns the wheel

The wheel levers the tiller and is attached to the rudder

The rudder maneuvers the ship like a shark fin

Fine establishment you've got here

Her? Oh, she's my sister

Sinister machinations of governing classes

Classy napkins on mechanical ships

Monocled blips and their designs

Designate your rights

To your right, the chancellor twists the proverbial spigot

The proverbial spigot clinches it for her allies

And all I got was this T-shirt

Shirts are a wardrobe essential

Essentially, I ignored the call

Call me anytime at: 0049 163 1828 198

I hate traipsing in iron gondolas in the middle of the night

Might we get out of this mess

Miss? I think you dropped some coins

Coincidence? I think not

Knots (mathematical variety) mark the way

Whey's the fluid rudiment that remains from the curds

"Hurdles like these are to be expected," the administrator articulated

A cuticled seashell shrinks in the sand

And with a little bit of glitter you can sell it for top dollar

Dollar, I said, but I meant to say Euro

Europe, the continent

Content am I

Eyes boring holes in a half-timbered house

Housing is a nightmare

A nightmare I had last night: Vultures picked at my chantilly lace top

Atop of which I donned an orange woolen sweater

Swearing, the birds squished silkworms in their enameled beaks

Bespeaking the moment's sentiment

Sediment collects itself

A shelf of tripods beside a twinkling body of liquid

Liquefied natural gas

Guess it all started with my ill-fitting shoes

Sure, she said, collecting her thoughts on a sinking ship

Ships are sovereign

Rein it in, ladies

Legs will only get you so far

Furthermore, you are not a special agent of change

Change is a declension, you know?

No. I do not … at least not precisely

Concisely: Mean is not medium is not meridian is not average

In a rage I scampered along a leafy footpath,

Took a bath

Bathed in the sea of frightening possibility

Proximity eased difficulty

Epistrophe appeased fairness

I far less preferred

To defer to a particle-board world covered with peanut shells

Shill an Andrew Jackson for a dinner

Son, you're a sinner

Singer's abasement = "Having cause to feel shame"

Same. I am comparatively well-off

Well, off you go, scampering to the walled medieval city

Citizens of all lands

Landed gentry

Gentlemens' clubs

Clubs with handles, like the delicate areas of the neck

Heck, I'm in Lübeck

Lübeck is known for its almond marzipan (among other things it is known for)

Four score and several years ago ...

Ego, the jovial one ...

Au passant one ...

Once you see it ...

It was all in an award-winning commercial

Commercial ships ferried soldiers and their arms

Arms attached to shoulders

Soldiers creak against the boards of the frigate

Rivet at the bane of my existence

The bane of my existence

My existence's bane

Bay window

Precursor

Two versions of the same thing

Even back then
the weather was
weird, she was
saying, and the
zeppelin, which
had somehow
made it to the
village, dangled
three hours
above it, and
when the sky
went chartreuse
(coterminous
with a
temperature
change) it
slurped it up like
root beer in a
twisty straw at
the pizza parlor,
until it floated
away and up into
the forest, where
light snowfall
weighed it down
and its
passengers
(journalists,
illustrious
individuals who
had traveled far
to admire this

aerial   device)
parlayed   out
with ropes from
the   trees   the
zeppelin   had
settled   on.
Nobody   died.
There's   a
placarded   rock
in   the   forest
commemorating
this mishap, this
was   prior   to
zeppelins
explicitly
connoting
warcraft,   there
was ambient and
genuine
excitement
surrounding the
prospect   of
human   beings
afloat in the sky
in   ovaline
devices and not
relegated   to
baskets   and
proximate to the
hot   air   fire,
instead
languorously

ambling around
between tables
like   bipedal
rocks,   like
everything's
highly   normal.
Today they only
exist   in   the
abstract. There's
a shrimpy silver
zeppelin sticking
out of the former
Riesling   bottle
on   the   birch
commode
siphoning my
"sleeping   area"
from where I
hang   damp
clothes. I needed
a trinket to take
for the road, to
signify   I   was
there. Alternate
thing: cloth
entrails.
Sometimes, my
clothes are super
crumbly, I'm too
lazy   to   shake
them out. The
polkadotted and
turquoise
ironing   board
behind them just

gathers damp, and it is ovaline, akin to the zeppelin. Did I mention I was in the bath? Yes, she was telling me all this when there was splashing in the background, my pale toes squiggling in alkaline H_2O, thus especially soothing. At this point she cuts me off because she needs to go on a jog before it gets too hot outside, it's so important to get exercise these days, keep it moving, move around

Torgau

Onward and upward

>The Renaissance stair

Wound around a newel

>Insinuating like a pendulum

On impassive sandstone where

>Allied forces

Said their hellos

>Mere yards from the brown bears

Probably sleepy

>In the waterless depression

Through which an attacker might

>Scramble like an avatar

Dressed in loins

>Belly-up in the bedroom

Belly-down for the lumbar

>Twinge which luckily

Has its killers

>But thanks to the padded shorts

Everywhere I sit's a seat

>The center of the world

Which responds to my sensitivities

>Even potential ones

Which I worry like a gossip

>Which I tear like a scab

Which I tender for under

>30 EUR/hour

Tracy and I plotted it

>Extending my palm like the antipode

In his improbable garb

>Five ghostly children

Castigate the epitaph

>Who is their father

One celebrity beside them

        Doing things properly by the well

Which reminds me:

        Do you know Katharina

Or any of her children

        I don't but send her my best

Regards and bet she cast her eyes

        Down at the brown bears

Before the terrible accident

        One and the same

I advise you to look up

        Fall back asleep if you need it

If it takes three months of this,

        So be it

Worth Home

Do you know where the ceremony is? No

              Do you know what is depicted there

On the ceiling

              Where the ceremony is? It looks strangely affectionate

By that I mean a Bavarian-looking Joseph is

              Chit-chatting with the Pharaoh

It's all in Genesis

              And in Rhineland-Palatinate, ogle it

That half-figure atlas creeping

              Up the gilt stucco like the monarch

Whose chin collapsed into his fluffy collar

              Or the boyfriend who barreled

Into the tablet of Kalamatas to sturdy himself

              These things are taxing

They cost time, money, and dedication

              And the 12th-century knights who bequeathed the land

Looked at the land and bequeathed it

              Then shut up about it

Don't laugh

              The order propped

Itself up in choir chairs

              And didn't wear underwear, and didn't speak

And today we are meant

              To be charmed by this and are dutiful.

This is beautiful,

              Everyone bloviates, hustled to the antechamber

Where there isn't any dancing (despite it being feasible)

              The box that canoodles easy jazz

Is conical and obviously

              Adjusted by a vase

Gardenias are filling

              How's your baby? I won't ask

I won't even speak to you

                              I won't even tape my third and fourth toes
Together like the life hack

                              And when someone snorts, won't
Cede while I in my stilettoed

                              Self remain cool
As the bride in her taffeta boatneck

                              Glistens to math jokes
Me? Oh, sure I've got plenty

                              Really
Same goes for years

                              That's parity, baby
We're two peas in a pod

                              I'm taking my makeup off and I'm sorry
It's been a long and consequential day

Way of the Walls

1. So that was that
2. On vacation
3. Entertaining
4. Supreme ease
5. Like a delicacy
6. Nobody tastes
7. Definitely no
8. Orange zest
9. Warped in dough
10. I'll never forget
11. That its severer
12. Was so friendly
13. But didn't register
14. How it works
15. I don't bat an eyelid
16. Everyone's been so sick
17. Here's where your antecedents
18. Fetched wood, Patricia
19. Warmed selves
20. Silkwormish
21. Or dozed without
22. In a humid enclave
23. Of the free
24. Museum admission
25. Where luminaries flank
26. Neutral walls
27. And are honored
28. Just like a passable
29. Charging bull
30. A line perspires
31. To grab some of
32. It's highly specific

33. With inspiration from Frankfurt
34. A quadricentennial
35. Commemoration
36. And its corollary
37. A scaffolded
38. Walkway to enshrine
39. Every column has an order
40. Every order, a classicism
41. This one is Corinthian
42. And not austere
43. Unlike the Tuscan
44. Beneath which it seems
45. "Christians are to be taught"
46. I was the comedic lead
47. Turning pinkish
48. "Christians are to be taught"
49. Something like that
50. Moneyed youth
51. But not on me
52. "How vain it is to trust"
53. A sect I met
54. Whereby I live
55. Both of them bespectacled
56. And I, polite
57. Apologized
58. Enacted what I thought
59. I liked about
60. That country
61. A gratuity of purpose
62. Picking words from a song
63. Says he'll
64. Have my baby

65. To a perfect stranger

66. Which I was to her

67. And she to me

68. Who lugs

69. 70 pounds of luggage

70. Down stoop

71. To sidewalk

72. No one is wrong

73. Statements are

74. And, sure

75. I'll have a scoop

76. Wager two steps

77. Gaze to the player

78. A slick vehicle

79. Plus its purveyor

80. Diffuse like the gauze

81. I wrapped around

82. My missing tooth

83. 12 years ago

84. The child that knocked

85. On the door

86. Can I have my CD

87. Back, she asked

88. I was too

89. Woozy to answer

90. Walked around the mall

91. Then thought

92. Better of it

93. Anything is causal

94. It all takes place

95. Here and now

Lakes in Brandenburg

Patently

Obvious like a push pin

Or lichen

Beyond the lake sextuplet

And then in a grotto

That tears

Up like a Luddite

Who winces as she saunters

In the German salon

Doing a good deed

For the state

Library while her boyfriend

Is filmed walking

Into the dusty foyer

But not out of it

And they're both asked

When they're leaving the bus

With all their stuff

Mildly annoyed

Then there's this tiny hole

Big enough to swim in

Not like the residue

The little sticker left

If only it would rain

And the hole would fill

And then a raft

Would float

Hapless

Deliver goods

Like brass tacks, or prune plums

Then arrive at the shore

To recollect

Our taxes like a tool

        I pay twice

And am transferred

        And wait very long

To approve the transfer

Proposition

1. Napoleon met with Goethe to talk about Werther
2. While she lay on her bed
3. Certainly, it must have happened like this
4. Anyone can do what has already been done
5. There it is: the amber tankard
6. The hypothetical lifts to his parched lips
7. And yet everyone tends to it
8. The unpolluted water and its ingredients
9. The toilet bowl needs to be cleaned weekly
10. The green sandstone is local to the region
11. The edifices in the city
12. Are now "so pretty." Just like before
13. There was a hot air balloon
14. Sponsored by an electricity provider
15. Inflating, then taking flight
16. And its onlookers so rapt at its fragility
17. Everyone clapped when it floated off
18. It became obvious our friend was embroiled in a property dispute
19. With his own (pardon the expression) flesh and blood
20. The chimney sweeper shook his consternated head
21. When you were children you called each other pet names
22. But everything worked out in the end
23. Exonerating both to HAVE A NICE REST OF YOUR DAY
24. In which she ruminated but could not floss
25. She had been thoughtless, selfish and cruel
26. She was recombinant on a pebbled beach by the Adriatic Sea
27. Water is healing, so she waded shin-deep in it
28. Marched around a rectangular pool like a stork
29. The question was first if and then how she was able to change
30. Then the shriveling plastic on the stovetop
31. A concomitant fungus
32. When self-scanning the red paprika

33.   She was asked if she still wanted it

34.   Apologized and said well no, not anymore

35.   And so it was retrieved to a plexiglass domain

36.   It was so appealing: to think it all might work out in the end

37.   Man I love a vista, she said, swinging from the citadel

38.   On which there was a swing set

39.   In some areas, it was a noxious, stinking weed

40.   In others, it was cultivated, harvested, dried, pulverized

41.   Soaked in a vat with ammoniac urine

42.   This led to the town's astonishing wealth, but also its decline

43.   Though in the possession of plenty of coins, she had none of the proper currency

44.   On her way home she gathered empirical knowledge

45.   Wondered at stains on the pavement

46.   Her onward progression through it

47.   As she stood in line to buy sandwiches and devour them on the meridian

48.   There was no way around but through traffic

49.   She kept the pencil after that: It was small and had no eraser

50.   In the letter she was a white petunia clutching a Bible to her chest

51.   A veneer of the past on whatever could shoulder it

52.   Paradigmatic alignment and apply it to the face

53.   As one would a chemical sunscreen

54.   Going on all protrusions, like a nose it is obvious

55.   In lieu of a better use of your wads of cash

56.   She and her mother, mulling in the café (trays with couscous salads on them)

57.   A display reminds its readers potatoes were taken from the Americas

58.   And at the buffet: 9 Euro Salzkartoffeln. The next-best decision elided them

59.   A boat wedged in a channel, all its accruing costs

60.   Their intimacy bartered with, like a higher power, or a judge

61.   Same with their transgressions

62.   Whose judgment fell like a Douglas fir

63.   A log cabin

64.   Therefore the treasures of the gospel are nets

65.   Nets with which one now fishes for the wealth of men

66.   Reifying the car's need of a wash

67.   A pleasurable jaunt through tinted soaps

68. As Nancy unwedged boat from the sandbar
69. And clung to a branch to steady herself
70. When her sweatshirts were sorted some had large stains of blood
71. There's no way we'll ever know
72. I was a historical guide, but I explained it wrong
73. It made no difference, then did
74. Actually, the man breathlessly intervened
75. There used to be bowling alleys here
76. But before that it was a castle
77. That was the iteration they were going with now
78. A politician said the city deserved to be "pretty"
79. Especially in its famous islet
80. And yet we find ourselves here today
81. When they spotted a German Shepherd
82. My grandparents were quick to identify it
83. They got along with their counterparts
84. If not for totally innocuous reasons
85. It was the appearance of tolerance
86. Now they're all dead
87. So there to, Grandpa Ken would say
88. His resignation
89. To have resigned what was past
90. As he hustled us into the red pickup to drive off from the sandbar
91. Nancy stood out back and cued him left, right, left, right
92. The chairs in which they sat have not disappeared but cleaved
93. There is a kindergarten being built where there was a blacksmithery
94.
95. The banister on the wall has detached for some reason

Revolution

I feel dizzy

        Imbuing my good

With argument

        So that it becomes a cabinet

In which to fold cloth

        Contentious

Inventing things

        But doesn't it tut

Value-neutrally

        Proceeding

To sip water

        And thence continuing its activity

Sheer coincidence

        Like a child scooping sand

Inside his tee

        Not realizing it is precious

However acutely he is

        As breakfast was cookies with stars

That submerge in warm milk

        You undunk like a ligament

Biding an hour on Saturdays

        At McDonald's

Until you're in the dimly lit

        Kitchen with an ulterior

Steam function

        Or at the festival in which the combustion

Engine never happened

        But a man nods at us convivially

Strolling with his compatriot

        As I enjoy a processed almond

Rapid inflation

        Tasked local alchemists

To figure out porcelain

        It wasn't the same

As what they had purchased

        You can pull it from the fire

Plunge it into a vat of ice

        Mark it with your two swords

With blue ink

        Trust me

Nothing will happen

        Then anything can

Central Oregon

1. I stood somewhere in the ponderosas.
2. A single trickle of sap emitted from them.
3. My great-great-grandfather owned several sawmills in the area.
4. Recreated here.
5. His son, perhaps, a notorious worker at the ketchup factory.
6. Perhaps that which was shrouded in mystery had actually been abundantly clear—we simply refused to see it.
7. Including the legitimacy of the son, the son's son, his various cousins, his children, his children's children, me.
8. Throughout the state of Oregon.
9. Some of whom showed up at the funeral.
10. That was when she saw them for the very first time.
11. Oh my god, you exist!
12. Then tore off a giant piece of garlic bread.
13. Ha ha, said his wife—weren't you on an elimination diet?
14. Worms squirreling in the rainforest.
15. The work of a beaver, in an embankment.
16. The work of a nutria, behind the peach orthodontist's.
17. You can see it by the salmon river.
18. His utilitarian teeth.
19. A truly majestic man-made dam.
20. Onlookers stopping their cars.
21. And emerging from them: a bald eagle!
22. A jogger, out of breath: I hope you have a great day!
23. His persistence in drought.
24. The birds of prey aren't flying today, the greeter tells us—though their presence is not as morally repugnant as you may think.
25. This fox? We found him mangled by the side of the road and lovingly restored him.
26. This bald eagle? Well, his left wing has something wrong with it.
27. So you can see him thoughtfully through the glass.
28. Reassured, we nod.

29. What news at the realtor's?

30. Four bedroom, three bath, killer deal.

31. Our seller is highly motivated, the realtor says, you won't see one like this again.

32. If you'd like to up your equity, she continues.

33. Which everybody should.

34. Friend … Enemy … Friend again.

35. (Referring to the birds of prey.)

36. Alive with plants … and animals.

37. (…)

38. Well, the realtor was nice, and she gave me an emerald-white pamphlet with suggestions for someone who might repair the garbage disposal.

39. Not that kind.

40. You mean you can pour your food down the sink? Johannes asked, incredulous.

41. Here, he goes by Joe.

42. Well, you could.

43. He's getting over something, so we amble up the hill.

44. Slowly.

45. Time is of the essence.

46. We take it all in until we can't anymore.

47. So do I, cantering on a horse.

48. The horse is like the beagle, it whinnies.

49. The beagle is like the horse, it's spotted.

50. Spotted: another bald eagle!

51. Or no· a spotted owl in the barn, swooping.

52. Or looking fluffy and dormant.

53. The climbers on the cliff: they did all that with their grip.

54. Behind them, a dormant volcano called Black Butte.

55. My parents discuss hiking up it.

56. You have to know where to look, and where to turn off in case your tensor fasciae latae tears,

57. And then make 10-mile journey towards the gravel road.

58. Her rescuer was so angry. Nobody knew why.

59. The neighbor chatted us up as we heaved our bikes in the truck.

60. Everything's all better now.

61. I was walking towards this neighbor when I saw his tremendous garage.

62. It was utterly incongruous with the region.

63. I paused.

64. On the other hand, the treasure of indulgences is naturally most acceptable, for it makes the last to be first.

65. Then continued forward to my door.

66. Children rang its bell and ran away.

67. I imagined a scenario in which I confronted the neighbor, asking: Why?

68. Politely.

69. In fact, there is no such thing as effective communication.

70. The pallet of bread dissolving in my mouth, and the grape juice that hasn't been fermented.

71. Luckily, despite my baptism, I haven't had to pay the taxes.

72. Clerical error.

73. Consult dad: He is the expert.

74. Also the Protestant.

75. Everyone is free to do as they like in this country.

76. It's the best system of all bad ones, says Dad.

77. Out for a bike ride, huh?

78. We drove to where there were fewer cars, and my gloved hands baked in the sun.

79. You think everything will be like this.

80. In retrospect, it won't be.

81. Well, it's totally within his rights, said Dad.

82. You can hear people go up and down the stairs.

83. You can hear my mother whisper in conspiratorial tones.

84. The most expensive part of the house to recarpet.

85. The most expensive hobby available to me is downhill skiing.

86. I was flying, I wrote in my diary.

87. Literally flew, tumbling down the icy corduroy.

88. One ski up top, the other below me. Bob slid down to help me out.

89.   Though it happened to me, I can only guess at what happened.

90.   I fell with complete equanimity at my fate, calm.

91.   For days, a thumb of my neck remained stiff—my left side.

92.   I extended my hands to mimic the spread of a California condor and tipped my head to my right.

93.   Of which there were so many—now only nine, if my memory serves me.

94.   Again, they are raised in captivity.

95.   Their captors confident of their entry into heaven.

Walden Pond

Some   dad
recorded   his
baby's   gurgles
and set them to
the   tone   of
"Thunderstruck."
I wondered how
much time it took,
seized my luck,
had a beer and
followed it up
with   some
strawberry sorbet.
Ah, summer. Life
is what happens
when   you
remember May
2012   in   pure
dread and fear.
Life is also what
happens   when
you say "I simply
cannot deal" and
defer,   tuck
spaghetti
bolognese   in
napkins, I'm truly
excellent at that. I
was living apart
from
companionship,
in the sense I had

decided to divest
from that of
which I was part.
Then I realized
"Damn, that's
fucked up" and
ruminated,
chewed on grass
like a lilac cow in
the Alps. Except
then I was in
Washington
State. Things
change so
incredibly
quickly. That
accent's not from
here, but hardly
anything is. The
issue with so
many contrarians
is with everyone
with a bone to
pick a bone to,
there are no bones
left. It's best to
pluck pink
rhododendrons on
the sand
peninsula with
green kitchen
scissors and pray

the inevitable
tsunami won't
wash it all away.
It would be too
bad for Jake the
Alligator Man, a
papier-mâché (?)
allegory for how
we are never just
one thing. My
father never
divested from this
fully either, but
for when the
laminate tiles
literally shifted
on this peninsula
we were on, and
our neighbors
screamed at us
from the bed of
the truck. "We're
fine," yelled my
father, just totally
gone. His brother
Bob showed me
how tectonic
plates work with
the palms of his
hands. Nothing he
said was false. I
went outside and
tap-danced on
wooden planks, I
sang along to

"Singing in the
Rain" in the rain.
I slipped out,
that's what I hear,
on my bum. I
looked up from
my book.

Chestnut Avenue

X marks the spot

Go my forearms

Like an ideogram

In a purple shirt

Who is repetitive

Like predatory snails

Who secreted

Ink by altercating

No, I'm listening

Apportioned

Multiple Tupperwares

Of us taking cues

In rectangles

Of mint foam

And papyrus

Enunciations like a tulip

Who holds its shape

Cutely

When someone says get the fuck

Out of my sight, OK

But don't, honestly

Know what it means

And so recollect

My taxes like a nod

That's free to individuals

Together in a bracket

Like on Sunday in the

Avenue beside music

Where I had a sampler

With Lindsey

And it only occurred

To me then

So what if

                    He was wearing long sleeves

Then a tank top

                    Or he was wearing

A thick, white cloth

                    Glove

What it hid

                    Nobody knows

Metropolitan

1.   So do you read literature?
2.   Yeah.
3.   Placated and ventilated
4.   In the room's relative dimness,
5.   She waited for the moment
6.   To pass.
7.   Then they saw the medieval
8.   Knights, whose armor
9.   Did not seem comfortable.
10.   Would you like something
11.   To eat?
12.   Yeah, indefinitely.
13.   She practiced hinging at the hips
14.   To correct
15.   A historical inaccuracy, the
16.   Hypermobility of the spine.
17.   A man tipped his forehead on
18.   A window frame, next
19.   Had difficulty finding words.
20.   I still had these problems
21.   With my alveoli,
22.   She informed the doctor …
23.   What else do you need to know?
24.   He shrugged.
25.   She never saw him again.
26.   Nothing is quite analogous.
27.   The problem was amorphous.
28.   Data accretes like an island
29.   In Scotland!
30.   Everybody wants to buy.
31.   Even her
32.   Stern nurse.

33. She had asked for assistance

34. The predictable thing occurred.

35. On the angle of a felt

36. Mountainside called

37. "Chimney Rock"

38. Her boyfriend began to slip ...

39. It wasn't just the lack

40. Of proper footwear.

41. Walking poles

42. Afforded him stability

43. On the mound of dirt

44. Which implied the ground

45. Like sulfuric ash.

46. And it was.

47. It's good to have a purpose,

48. An end goal,

49. His guide firmly stated.

50. When your refrigerator breaks,

51. It's good to have a job

52. Even if it entails

53. Buying a new refrigerator

54. And then the old one rares

55. Up again.

56. Let's go through the American

57. Wing and then to ancient Egypt,

58. Where they filmed

59. That scene.

60. Two lovers reunite.

61. Are you in the elevator?

62. Yeah.

63. Oh, that's where?

64. Go outside, she urged.

65.   Look.

66.   Every man is wearing

67.   Brown leather mules.

68.   Hard not to notice the

69.   Sulfuric smell

70.   With no effect

71.   On said leather mules.

72.   Every millisecond

73.   Value is processed.

74.   · Every millipede possesses

75.   Numerous legs

76.   And scuttles in like an elevator

77.   Or toilet paper

78.   A white American child

79.   Like Goldilocks

80.   Looks around

81.   Her arms

82.   In every luxury campground

83.   With unlimited sinks.

84.   Among other tabulations of

85.   Wealth and value.

86.   It all happens on the inside,

87.   And yet it's worthless

88.   If you don't perceive it.

89.   On the other hand, they X-rayed

90.   My lungs just once,

91.   And on the phone,

92.   Told me

93.   They didn't find anything of

94.   Note

95.   Besides lungs, of course.

Door 1

It starts with the drive back from the hospital. Who's driving the car? Who chose the music? Who's picking up their dog shit? Who unraveled the spigot? Who's playing the drums? Who's holding up the line? Who's cozy in their living rooms? Who watches a woman stretch homemade mozzarella? Who cut the ribbon? Who even likes that sort of thing? Who bought that for you? Who has that kind of money? Who cares? Who's cleaning up after her? Who is the insistent pedagogue? Who gave herself the gift of a ceramics class? Who took his children to Applebee's? Who leafed through the brochure? Who read the terms and conditions? Who jumped 12 feet high? Who? Who called it "Swiss" cheese? Who is neutral like a knife? Who ticked the box? Who said nothing? Who ascends the cliff and bumps her head? Whose throat is hurting? Whose isn't? Whose name is on the street sign? Who looks at membranes under a microscope? Who invented stenography? Who said necessity was the mother of invention? Who tumbles down a mountain? Who cuts her arm on a branch? Who assures her subjects of safety? Who calls the mountain the mountain? Who parcels it? Who can imitate bird sounds? Who's ever shot a gun here? Who here is a doctor? Who thinks I'm pretty? Who has ever eaten caviar? Who took the last slice of Gruyère? Who has demurred to her employer? Who is chewing gum so loudly? Who knew that there was plastic in that? Who clings to that social position? Who was born in a certain station? Who visits us? Who has registered to vote? Who is good at this sort of thing? Who has cultivated a mystique? Who won't shut up? Who finances this? Who is subject to the whims of fate? Who's financed by it? Whose style is marked by a certain ... finesse? Who didn't think she would enjoy it ... then did? Who relaxed in a recliner? Who took a speeding train to Innsbruck? Who traces the tender progression of time? Who considers herself a historian? Who determines that? Who's there? Who hurt her knees? Who tenderly pokes his puckered skin? Who did that to you? Who believes in that? Who's envious of her? Of him? And then, the baby? Who thinks of the baby? Who sends the baby to the opera? Who leads the baby opera group? Who wrote the program? Who typed it out? Who passed it out? Who repeated it? Who fainted? Who's in charge here? Who knows how to fix this? Who can tell me the answer? Who hears the baby crying? Who can take care of it? Who knows what is going on? Who slathers his bread in butter? Who has to live with that decision? Who knows what will happen?

The Patricians

Preamble

Very little is happening.

In fact, look around you. It's like this every day.

*Put your deodorant where you use it, not where you put it. That's what **SOMEONE** always says.*

It's all so consequential, always leading to something else.

It's like this string that holds up the shower curtain, which is attached to the lighting. It's dental floss.

*And sometimes, after showering too much, it falls off. It's not coincidental, **JOHANNES** notes, that this only happens when **YOU** shower: **YOU'RE** kind of jerky.*

*Three **PATRICIANS** sip from pearlescent flutes. In a surprise turn, **BRAD** has been dumped from the Island. The **PATRICIANS** reflect on the hand they have been given.*

*There's a homunculus inside **YOU**. Its name is your name.*

*It arms and predates **YOU**. It's a whitish and phlegmy creature.*

*Sometimes it intuits things that aren't there. Or that things are wrong, when they aren't, everything's fine, **PATRICIA**.*

*You know how **YOU** can hear someone breathing?*

*Even when **YOU'RE** in another room in the house?*

Everything desultory of if … then …

Act 1, Scene 1

It is so obvious who it is.

It is the first day of vacation, and **SOMEONE SPECIAL** *has come to visit.*

It is **URSULA.** **SHE'S** *just awoken from a nap, jet-lagged and sleepy. Via a series of events* **WE** *tread a shallow eddy in the river. Then a rectangle with cold water named after its inventor,* **ALFRED KNEIPP.**

WE *wade in that like storks.*

Then put on our socks.

Then walk back to the apartment.

Act 1, Scene 2

Several instances pass, in which **WE** *ascend and descend three stories.*

URSULA *and* **THERESA** *share a primordial bond.* **THEY** *were born a single year apart.*

THEY *notice:* You have something under your nostril.

THEY *notice:* You aren't particularly well-dressed.

THEY *notice:* You have a spot on your jeans. What is that? Chocolate?

THEY *have decided to take a road trip and doze while the car charges its battery.*

A battery of X ...

The **PEASANTS'** *uprising of the Y ...*

It all comes to a T ...

Let the **LEISURE CLASSES** *stiffen their collars ...*

Act 1, Scene 3

Now listen to **ME** *for a moment.*

It is possible to feel **YOUR HEART** *beat against* **YOUR WILL.**

Sometimes, **YOU** *can do so in* **YOUR LEFT EAR DRUM**. *Though it is irregular.*

One is in the heart of a region that thinks of **ITSELF** *as having appendages, which all behave in cohesion. Tee hee hee.*

Thump thump thump.

Now inflect this with the memory of **ALL** *those* **YOU** *have wronged.*

No time to apologize: Move on.

. . .

If there is no place to backtrack to, let it be a recreation.

It's precipitating. **YOU** *might cover your crown, but your bench will get wet.*

I hope you enjoy this complimentary muffin, **SOMEONE** *mutters.*

URSULA *wipes her mouth with a cloth napkin:* Thank you so very much!

It's tradition. This really happened.

Act 1, Scene 4

It's tradition. This really happened. **THEY** *had no money for the building. That's where* **THE DEVIL** *came in.* **THE DEVIL** *espied the building (which would become the church) from the vantage there were no windows in. From where* **THE DEVIL** *was standing, there were no windows, neither stained nor translucent. That was* **HIS** *condition: That there was daylight, but that it did not flood in the church. Then, on inauguration day,* **THE DEVIL** *took a single step forward.* SLAM! *That's where* **THE DEVIL** *came in:* **HE** *saw the windows as the angle drenched the edifice with ambient light.* **HE** *was so angry,* **HE** *took a step forward.*

Act 1, Scene 5

URSULA: There it is: Your foot fits in it.

Pre-war, there were medieval windows here. Post-war, **PATRICIANS** *ambled downtown and purchased Andalusian accouterments from* **A SALESMAN** *on the road.*

It's like nothing ever happened. **THE ARCHITECT** *breathed in deeply and delighted in his cruel trick.*

ME: The salesman did not know what part of Andalusia, exactly, this garlic peeler was from: He was only selling it.

Today there is a long line in front of TK Maxx, so **URSULA** *and I nix it.*

ME: And mailing packages occupies so much psychic energy that I do not do it.

YOU *don't need* **ME** *to tell you the moral of the story.*

Act 1, Scene 6

SOMEONE'S MOTHER transports us to a trip on the river

On which SOMEONE was so restless

SHE paced on the steamboat, which was scenic

Or turned mere passage into scenery

And SHE too, SHE was scenery

To THOSE taking photos of the river.

Even on this river, which reminds one of another river, THEY have steamboats.

...

The VOICEOVER called ALL to look at their lefts, if facing the stern, and consider that yellow sanatorium atop a hill.

In that very sanatorium, some FOURTEEN THOUSAND were killed.

EVERYONE shifts in their wooden benches.

VOICEOVER: Our next stop is a beautiful castle where you can listen to string quartets.

EVERYONE shifts in their wooden benches.

Act 1, Scene 7

YOU can't run away forever.

Remember those things ***YOU*** *did, half asleep?*

THESE FORCES *are, admittedly, congruent.*

At some point ***WE*** *removed ourselves from the boat and scurried to the top of the sandstone formations.*

It was so beautiful, ***WE*** *didn't know what to do with it.*

. . .

Just like the knowledge of cruelty and its implication.

URSULA: I wonder what it was called before.

WE licked our ice cream cones.

ME: My mother enjoyed lemon sorbet.

URSULA: But her scoop was a brighter hue.

Act 1, Scene 8

PATRICIANS are murmuring. This all feels so familiar.

WE were let off at the bottom of the hill and then WE walked up it. This all feels so familiar.

First WE walked through some stick-like woods and then there was a field. This all feels so familiar.

PEOPLE wear socks without soles here.

THEY only cover their shins.

THEY slap their thighs and stand up from things.

THEY exclaim: Not ME! Look next door! That's who YOU'RE looking for! This all feels so familiar.

One ENGLISH-SPEAKING WOMAN marched up and made her case.

This all feels so familiar.

THEY sat and slurped spaghetti ice cream while discussing this.

It was impossible to clear the look of disgust from her face.

What flavor did SHE get?

Act 1, Scene 9

URSULA wrings her hands. SHE clears out the dishwasher and misplaces every-thing. THERESA is possessed by the rectangle on which SHE patterns candy in rows of three.

What visions dance in YOUR HEAD?

Do YOU intend to sleep?

I'm sure they prepared for all possible contingencies, SHE says, irritated by the tinge of despair in HER voice.

A historic paradigm shift is taking place. Everything continues on as it has been. The chaos at the airport can't be captured in photographs, but the PATRICIANS do their best to imagine it, then scuttle the thought from their heads. The departure is approaching and colors everything.

Act 1, Scene 10

EUROPEAN CENTRAL BANK: Will the euros in your pocket buy you as much tomorrow as they do today? Can you rely on your bank in good times and bad? There are 4,000 of us working here at the ECB to make sure the answer to these questions is a resounding yes!

YOU should get that mole checked out, or perhaps removed. YOU don't want to deal with the consequences.

URSULA: Let me see it? Bring the camera closer.

Sometimes they freeze them off. YOU don't even feel it. Or perhaps that's a wort.

And sometimes there's a scar, but that's better than the alternative, *HER SISTER says, forebodingly.*

Act 1, Scene 11

That's how it went.

Or how it's going, rather.

*In order to survive, **WE** need: **FOOD, SHELTER,** and **WATER**.*

***SOMEONE** hugs her **LOVED ONES** at the airport. **SHE** holds them close. Unequivocally, **SHE** is crying. There is quite a bit of mucus involved. Luckily, her local pharmacy gives her tissues with every purchase. **SHE** reaches into her purse.*

End of Act 1

Act 2, Scene 1

SOMEONE'S MOTHER has long since left the country, but **HER MEMORY** presides.

HER departure makes way for romantic intrigue in which every **PATRICIAN** becomes individual.

It is only in the romantic endeavor that **ONE** *becomes* **ONE**.

There, a **LEOPARD**, *in pursuit of a mate.*

There, a **LADYBUG**, *on your elbow. Oops, now it's gone.*

SOMEONE *can open parcels, spill out their contents and throw them away. Or* **SOMEONE** *can wait for the* **NEIGHBOR** *to pick them up.*

This has been here forever, **HE** says, holding out medical-grade Vitamin A.

I'm sorry, I was at work, **SOMEONE** replies.

Act 2, Scene 2

From behind a luminescent wall **A PATRICIAN** *apprehends her love object.*

SHE *has a microphone in her ear. It's very intimate.*

Kneeling, **SHE** *narrates her knees being bruised in the gravel.*

Everything in the outside world will be different. It will relax, or it will adopt a disposition.

. . .

HER JOB: CAN YOU BELIEVE THIS, [[FIRST NAME]]?

This is an open-ended question.

Let's put a pin in it and move on.

HER JOB: CAN YOU BELIEVE THIS, [[FIRST NAME]]?

PATRICIAN: Ow! That pin is now in my foot!

Act 2, Scene 3

It is normal to wonder about the logical next step.

It could be there, where a single step has been trod.

ONE LITTLE CELL *wants* **THE BIGGER CELL** *to do well.*

It wishes the **CELL** *well because it needs the* **CELL** *to do well.*

In the stairwell, there's a suspicious shape. **SOMEONE** *won't spark the imagination to think of it.*

WE *were jumping on the trampoline, when* **HER 7-YEAR-OLD COUSIN** *became convinced of* **A SHAPE IN THE GRASS.**

Then convinced herself of it: **A NEFARIOUS SHAPE IN THE GRASS.**

Which became **AN EVIL ENTITY** *and* **WE** *comforted her.*

It must be noted, however, that **IT** *was never fully there.*

Act 2, Scene 4

IVAN: My physical therapist retrieved a package of dark-brown sludge from a drawer, which came wrapped in two parallel slips of A4-sized paper. She placed it on the disinfected chaise and wrapped my head in a damp terry-cloth towel. She looked expectantly at me and my unshirted torso.

There is a house being built. It is possible to walk around in its contours.

There is a faded soccer ball. It is quite deflated.

There is a meadow for the foreseeable future. WE will be able to look out to it from the island

For the next couple of years

There where there

Was a sandbox will be sand.

It has been averaged out.

WE meet to communicate or to visit funerals.

SOMEONE had a migraine and was unable to do either.

JULIA: Tim even has a car, his dad's Audi, I said we could pick her up if she wanted but I didn't hear back for 4 hours. Afterwards I got a text, check this out: 'sorry, I was asleep.' Yeah, right. I was crying my eyes out with her boyfriend, she saw my stories, I knew. Look, nothing happened, I was just super sad, nobody was there for me, I was alone in Tim's car with Tim.

Act 2, Scene 5

IVAN: When I knew you and your mother were waiting by my apartment, I got very antsy. After about 25 minutes, the package went cold. It was clammy and uncomfortable. I took a roll of paper towels I saw on the counter and wiped off the encrusted mud. I saw myself out and never returned to the office again.

The very next week, IVAN was unable to carry his head. He thought he was all better and had attempted a pull-up on the local calisthenics equipment, sponsored by Adidas. This did IVAN in.

JULIA: I got my leg sunscreen on the leather seats and Tim didn't even fucking blink. He was so good. But I'll remember that betrayal forever. Even when I'm in the middle of a field, and billy goats grazing, all I can think about is how I fucked up my wingliner that night. I was kayaking in my cascading tears, my lashes stand-up paddle boards for the saltwater squirting out of my eyeballs.

JULIA applies lipstick.

Firearms exploit the expansion of a gas.

I never thought about it that way, **SOMEONE** *says.*

Act 2, Scene 6

While we had been chatting, interest rates were being monitored and controlled.

WE *come into the world one way: helpless.*

SOMEONE'S MOTHER *(very hot):* I'm melting!

Act 2, Scene 7

Well, isn't that a fertile source of bitterness?

Why don't **WE** let sleeping dogs lie?

Well, there's my dog **FRITZI**. **SHE** was put to sleep.

YOU haven't lived until you've seen **A DOG LIKE HER** on a beach.

Specifically, Bandon Beach, in Oregon, the United States.

That's where **SOMEONE** has been.

Fishing for compliments in the bottom of the Pacific.

Peripatetic and taking deep breaths.

Moving deliberately, into optical flow.

The ocean is something amazing.

In low tide. These fluvial zones, they're like sediment.

I do not believe in God but I do in the sentiment.

It makes little deltas with it.

Confessions proliferated across the country. **FRITZI** began to whelp. The rock formations looked suspiciously like human faces. But **YOU** were not the first to think that.

On the contrary.

*I thought of **MY VIOLIN TEACHER**.*

Go to sleep and trip on something and wince.

Act 2, Scene 8

My brain can be redressed through play. Cute outfit.

Mistrust the X in lieu of the Y.

Red yellow orange blue green violet.

In an act of protest, perhaps the most radical one, **THE REFORMER** *presided over a decadent meal of sausages.*

THEY *walked past* **A STREET ARTIST** *sculpting a sand dragon with a friendly demeanor.*

THEY *walked back and gave that* **STREET ARTIST** *a coin.*

Come to think of it

It was the way

HE *smiled at* **HER**

*—***THE DRAGON OUT OF SAND.***

Act 2, Scene 9

SOMEONE *agrees to watch baggage from* **A PERSON**

SOMEONE *does not know*

Who needs a water bottle.

When **HE** *gets it,* **HE** *drinks a little, then spits it out.*

But **I**'*m getting ahead of myself.*

Act 2, Scene 10

Yes ... Yes ... Yes ... Yes ...

(This is the internal soliloquy to **THE STRANGE WOMAN** *stressed*

By the presence of **HER PROGENITORS**

And their **SIBLINGS.**

AMERICANS.*)*

Walden Pond

Economy

I'd like to perfect my technique,
Which I know is wanting

Though in order to do that, I'd need fresh
Hands on my sternum and my chest

Newborn babies learn
That when they are suffering, something

Alleviates it
And as they grow, that alleviation becomes causal

Whereas before it was diffuse
A lot with clover on it, and grass

Where I Lived, and What I Lived For

If something horrible's normal
Even great minds will struggle with it

Clutch their trembling hand
The other clutching the feather

That's not just any feather, however
It's John Hancock's

A Founding Father's
Vengeful feather

Hovering over the dead goose
It was plucked from

Reading

Having learned to sew I am still a
Bit superstitious

This is a common pathway ... See?
Look how our Reeboks have trammeled it

I consider myself an empath,
But every nostril has its limits

Grimace
Isthmus

Sounds

It is not an unalloyed good,
Taking part in traffic

It is rather like the weather
A gold coin and its nickel

Do you see the face on it?
It looks so familiar

I'd recognize that chin from everywhere, even
100 mph on Highway 99.

Solitude

I peel my clandestine orange off
In one elegant strip

It had very large pores inside its zest
For life which I squirted

On my face. Hey! Get your mind out of
The gutter

There are two small raccoons looking
Out of it, how adorable

Oh no
Now there is a terrifying creature there

Visitors

We are all social creatures
Above me there was a sound

A man sawing a birch slat with a handsaw
One story over the crown

Of my head
I'd like to know what the point of it was

The next day, a parakeet
Sat on a twig and peeped from its cage

I am pretty
Sure it was the same window

The Bean-Field

Everything is brand-new for an infant
Indicators emerge

From a specific historical situation
See that linden branch? With its knobs?

That's precisely what I am talking about. To be
Sure I've internalized

That I turned off the stove
More profoundly that I have not

And that it is highly likely
All my neighbors will die

The Village

There was banging behind the window
People were doing things there

Daily life is sacral
On a thousand-dollar chair

Presented with noise-canceling headphones
A woman collapsed

On the parterre
In one ear she heard a specific wavelength—in another

Another one. I hope
This isn't

Too onerous
Though it is likely

The Ponds

Oh, I'm highly compatible.
Here, pat me on the head: It's soft.

We humans are like thermostats.
Don't forget to turn the stove off.

The invisible chancellor
Rambles forth on the airwaves.

Nancy and Ken
(My dead grandparents)

Listen. They were deathly afraid,
But that's not the thing that killed them.

That's just the way it is
But I can't explain to you why.

Baker Farm

My other dead grandparents, Heinz and Hermine,
Had nothing to say to that.

Likely it was because they were not
Mutually intelligible.

Every month, a costumed baby animal
Is taken from the calendar and taped to the wall.

They are so adorable.
But they don't stay that way.

Higher Laws

My life has been astonishingly simple
I am aware.

There is residual inflammation
In the cavity of my chest.

But before I redress
The conch shells on my bedspread

I indulge in things
That need indulging.

Here, crack open
A peanut.

Let's expense
Lunch.

Brute Neighbors

Behold
A child

Make it stop
Crying

Now you are crying too
Well, that makes four of us

Fuck!
Now five of us

House-Warming

There's something so special about that noise
Something so recognizable

He wanted a specific crown on his head
It had to be octagonal

He posed on a chaise for the painter
Now repose, said the painter

He shifted his head ... So it was under his hand
Stilted on an armature ... But something glinted beneath it.

Former Inhabitants, Winter Visitors

Life is the ultimate good.
Think of a spider, webbed in its gooey web.

Or like a skein
Of yarn

From the Yarn Barn
I didn't think would be so expensive, honestly

But it's for my mother, she loves knitting
She wants to knit a sweater for me.

Winter Animals

More myths are true than not
If truth is

Inimical and anathema
Two BFFs and their misdoings

Last Lent I went
To Bavaria and laughed at the monks

I would like to
Today, but for what? And why?

My neighbor sighs
And touches her eyeballs when she meets me

They are an extension
Of her brain

The Pond in Winter

Johannes says: evidence is evidence
Made by evaluation systems

Very likely I failed my friendships
And failed to remember my failings

As soon as you get too big for your britches
It's a good feeling

Perhaps I have left them
They need to be let

Spring

While away, Grandma Nancy mailed me a bottle of Tums
And homemade croutons. I overindulged

It's all a question of what you can
Tolerate

Or what your stomach can
(Calcium carbonate)

Conclusion

What's good for the goose
Is good if you wander

On the carpeted premise
The moon landing was 100% real

Same goes for the smell
Of burnt toast

On the dormant volcano
It came from

Somewhere
Didn't it?

Addendum

I am gallivanting, a truly
Political human being

Admiring the impressions
That hound me like a Chihuahua

I once saw in the drive-through graveyard
On a jog when it came barking

I briefly hopped on a gravestone, afraid
Acutely aware of its teeth. It wouldn't stop

And so I
Jogged on

Door 2

Some believe people are born in purity and are corrugated as
life goes on. As the toil of daily life grinds its insistent thumbs
in the knots in our backs. As your face swallows the imprint of
the pleather bench. As the knots dissolve and become tolerable.
As it includes a convenient oval for you to breathe through. As
things are slowly beginning to turn around. As someone is
talking to you. As you followed the directions perfectly but
there is so much unexpected these days. As long as everyone
here acts in good faith. As you enjoy a delicate saunter home.
As a matter of fact, I am feeling sleepy. As everyone in the room
is singing. As you walk past the churchful chirping *A Mighty
Fortress Is Our God*. As they really believe that. As we speak,
the exchange rate is being monitored and controlled. As the
individual consumer can have an impact, you know. As soon as
this check clears. As the reformer toils at his wooden desk. As
usual, autonomous entities divvy up their spoils. As per our
custom, three wet leaves of spinach are removed from the
salad mix. As the average person wastes far too much food, the
technocrat tells me. As I get a final friendly prompt to pay my
fees before collections are sent. As the cries for change do not
cease, despite the new regime. As I lean my head against the
window. As collateral damage is calculated in. As I ignore both
incoming calls and letters on principle. As the individual
consumer has an impact, you know. As opposed to what? As I
take a risk on my enemies. As elected officials snap a friendly
pic. As you asked for it. As the rest of the road was blocked by
the authorities. As it wasn't really clear who was in charge. As
it seems like everyone needs a vacation. As the medical advice
has changed on this issue. As a dirge progresses too uptempo
for your liking. As you've prepared a healthy meal at home
and would just like to enjoy it in peace. As if! says the lovely
protagonist. As it becomes uncomfortably obvious. As the sun

is slowly setting. As it was unclear who she was talking to. As it was a foregone conclusion. As it wasn't. As you were. As a little bunny rabbit. As a familiar face. As a sleepy piece of bread on television. As a double entendre. As a jar of pasta sauce. As he winked at you. As you were trying to fall asleep. As the soccer players sing along. As the national rail system tore through the landscape. As a single tear droops down his cheek. As the house has become quite decrepit. As the mezzo's a half beat behind. As she bows to a roaring applause. As it's too late to do anything at this point. As that's what they always say. As everyone exchanges a glance around the table. As one person feels very left out. As the lights were lowered evocatively. As some believe the opposite, that we are squishy and refined. As a masseuse squirts some oil from a nearly empty bottle. As the slow realization turns to horror. As troops were paid in coins. As that was the necessity of the situation. As a candle flickers too close to the polyester. As Hans looks this up for me, confirming what I already knew. As I doubled back to make sure everybody was safe. As I'm no expert. As luck would have it, my former employer sat beside me in the library. As if by magic, someone sat between us. As she had changed so much and was hardly recognizable. As I left the building, I typed something into my phone. As she slumbered on the mattress. As I was cycling home. As far as she was concerned, it was not her responsibility. As nobody thought twice. As I was developing an aural sensitivity. As a matter of fact. As everyone stood up for a moment of silence. As we brought it up later. As far as I know, everything you've said is true. As if I were someone to trust on this. As if we were doing a trust exercise. As the saying goes